MALLARD PRESS

An imprint of BDD Promotional Books Company, Inc.,
666 Fifth Avenue, New York, N.Y. 10103

Mallard Press and its accompanying design and logo
are trademarks of BDD Promotional Book Company, Inc.

CLB 2340
Copyright © 1990 Colour Library Books Ltd.,
Godalming, Surrey, England.
Copyright © 1990 Illustrations: Oxford Scientific Films Ltd.,
Long Hanborough, England.
First published in the United States of America
in 1990 by The Mallard Press
Printed and bound in Italy by Fratelli Spada, SpA
All rights reserved.
ISBN 0 792 45030 2

· *Oxford Scientific Films* ·

BIRDS OF PREY

Ian Gray

MALLARD PRESS

Contents

*A bald eagle (previous pages) among
buttercups and lupins and
(left) soaring over Alaskan Mountains.*

1
What is a Bird of Prey?

Birds of prey are also called raptors, from the Latin, meaning "to seize" or "to plunder". This is a very apt name for these birds because they live by seizing, killing and eating the flesh of other animals or plundering the carcasses of dead animals for food. Although birds of prey look very different from lions, wolves, hyenas, crocodiles and sharks, they play the same role in nature.

Being a *predator* and killing other animals for food is not cruel. Birds of prey have to kill in order to live, and all predators help to keep the natural world in balance. If they were not around, the numbers of other animals would increase rapidly, the environment would become overcrowded and species would soon run out of food and die of starvation or disease. Predators kill some animals, usually the old, sick or very young which are easy to catch, so that many can live. This keeps the prey populations healthy

and leaves fit animals to breed and maintain the population.

Raptors are amongst the most spectacular birds in the world. Often they are big, powerful and very beautiful, but always they are wonderfully skilled fliers. Hunting raptors provide us with some of the most spectacular sights in the animal world, such as that of an osprey plunging into a lake to catch a fish, or a peregrine diving at 150 miles per hour toward a pigeon, or a magnificent golden eagle soaring over mountain crags searching for prey.

Birds of prey are killing "machines" – their bodies are perfectly designed by nature for the hunting and killing of other animals. They vary greatly in size, form and appearance, from the tiny, sparrow-size falconets found in Southeast Asia, which weigh just over an ounce and have a wingspan of six inches, to the huge Andean condors of the mountains of South America, whose weight tips the scales at thirty pounds and whose wingspan is over three feet. For the most part, these differences depend on the way they hunt for food and the prey species they catch. Yet birds of prey are remarkably similar in many of their features. Virtually all possess a hooked beak for tearing flesh, specialized legs and feet armed with talons to hold and kill prey, and large eyes with very accurate vision.

Left: a pair of bald eagles. This beautiful and powerful bird is the national symbol of the United States.

Facing page top: the bizarre-looking king vulture from Central and South America, showing its distinctive orange wattle. This bird feeds mainly on carrion, but will also catch snakes.

Facing page bottom: as day breaks, an Alaskan bald eagle snatches a chum salmon from under the beaks of two gulls.

2
Around the World

Throughout the world there are approximately 290 different raptor species which, as a group, are known scientifically as the Falconiformes. They can be further divided into five subgroups based on their evolutionary origins. These are: New World vultures (seven species), secretary birds (one species), ospreys (one species), falcons (around sixty species) and the eagles, hawks, kites, harriers, buzzards and Old World vultures, grouped together as *accipiters* (around 217 species).

Raptors are superb flyers, and the air presents few physical barriers to their movements. As a group, they are found on all the continents of the world except Antarctica, and in virtually all habitats – from the high arctic to the equator, from the harshest deserts to humid tropical rainforests, and from the seashore to the highest mountains. The only habitat they have failed to

The mighty steppe eagle, found in Africa and Asia, is the most common of all eagles.

exploit fully is the ocean. Some have a very limited distribution, such as the Mauritius kestrel, the rarest raptor in the world – there are only a few of these birds left on the Indian Ocean island of Mauritius. Others, such as the osprey, are found near water throughout the world, breeding in North America, Europe and Asia and spending their winters in South America, Africa and southern Asia.

The largest concentration of raptors is found in warm, relatively open country. On the grassy savannahs of East Africa, the prairies of North America and the steppes of Asia live most of the vulture species, alongside numerous eagles,

One of the largest falcons, the gyr falcon (left) is found in the high Arctic and is much favored by falconers because of its speed and grace. Below: perched high on a bluff overlooking the Kenyan savanna, a dark chanting goshawk keeps a lookout for lizards, its principal prey.

harriers and other hawks. In South America many raptors, including New World vultures, have adapted to life in the vast tropical forests found there. In the cooler climates there are fewer species, mainly comprising woodland hawks and buzzards, and many of these must migrate to warmer climates during the cold winters. Only a few species can survive in the Arctic, the most beautiful being the gyrfalcon, the largest of the falcons, whose plumage is completely white.

In recent times many species have moved into urban areas, attracted by the chance of easy food. Peregrine falcons now nest on the sides of cliff-like skyscrapers in several cities, feeding on the abundant pigeons that live in urban squares and parks. Kestrels also nest in many cities and can easily be seen as they hunt for sparrows and mammals on waste ground, while kites and vultures scavenge for carrion in the street garbage and landfills of cities throughout the world.

3
Designed to Kill

Birds of prey have feet specialized for striking and piercing prey, gripping it tightly when flying and holding it down while feeding. Each foot has four strong toes, three facing forward and one backward, and each is armed with a sharp, recurved claw or talon. Just as we close our hands to hold something, raptors can clench

their toes together to grip and crush prey. Raptors such as the sparrowhawk, which hunt quick agile prey, have long, slim legs and toes and needle-sharp, thin talons to reach out and grasp escaping prey. Others that hunt large, heavy prey have short, thick toes and broad, immensely strong talons. The harpy eagle, which kills small antelopes, has toes six inches long and legs as thick as a child's wrist.

One of the most obvious features of any raptor is its hooked beak, which it uses to tear flesh from its prey. Of all raptors, only falcons use their beaks to kill, nipping and crushing the neck of their prey. Like their feet, bill shapes of birds of prey depend on the type of job each bird has to do. The griffon vultures of Africa have

Above: a Ruppell's vulture displaying the long, broad wings on which it soars effortlessly on rising thermals over the African plains. Its head lacks feathers, which would become fouled when it feeds inside carcasses. The bateleur eagle (right) has very strong legs and powerful talons armed with sharp claws, used to catch and kill snakes, lizards and small mammals.

huge, stout beaks to rip open a carcass by tearing at the hide, so reaching the *entrails* inside. Yet the Egyptian vulture has a long, delicate beak (rather like a pair of tweezers) which it delicately uses to remove the last slivers of flesh from the bones of a dead animal.

We have all heard the expressions "the eyes of a hawk" or "eagle-eyed" applied to someone with good eyesight, and indeed all raptors, not just hawks and eagles, have remarkable eyesight. Their eyes are very large – a buzzard's are the same size as a grown man's – and this enables them to spot objects from great distances and with great clarity. The ability to focus on and detect faraway objects is called resolving power, and eagles' eyes have a resolving power eight times stronger than human eyes. This means they can spot a rabbit almost two miles away!

All raptors fly well, and some are able to perform spectacular aerial maneuvers. Some, like vultures, have very long, broad wings which

allow them to soar and spiral like a glider for hours on end, while hawks that hunt in woodland have short, very broad wings and a long tail – so equipped, they are specialized for fast flying and quick maneuvering. Falcons are renowned for their speed, being capable of diving onto prey at over 150 miles per hour – speeds made possible by their long, narrow, pointed wings and their aerodynamic, bullet-shaped bodies.

The huge, powerful wings of a bald eagle carry it high into the air over the Alaskan mountains.

4
The Raptor's Day

All raptors are diurnal, which means they are active during the day, although several species are active during the half-light of dawn and dusk. Before leaving their overnight *roosting* perch, raptors clean themselves by *preening* their feathers. Their activities start soon after dawn with a series of short, warm-up flights – they do not hunt until they have warmed up and are flying properly. Most birds of prey are such efficient hunters that they only need to hunt for a few hours a day, and usually they do not have to hunt every day – for example, a crowned eagle can kill an antelope large enough to keep it going for three or four days. Raptors can also easily do without food for considerable periods of time – two to three weeks in larger birds – without coming to any harm. This allows them to survive food shortages and periods of bad weather when they cannot hunt. After hunting and feeding they usually return to a regular perch to spend the night – vultures, for example, might fly a hundred miles back to their favorite cliff-face roost. At the roost they usually preen again and then fall asleep with their heads under one of their wings.

Above: a turkey vulture warms itself by stretching its wings to absorb the heat of the morning sun. Right: from its roost perch in a dead tree, an Alaskan bald eagle watches the moon rise.

5
The Raptor's Year

Some raptors live in the same place all year round – these are called residents – while others spend part of the year in varying regions of the world – these are called migrants and their movements migration. Most migrations are away from the cold weather of *temperate* and arctic winters, as during such times food is too scarce for the birds to remain; mammals *hibernate*, many small birds migrate, fish lie *dormant* in frozen lakes and insects become inactive. At these times raptors move to warmer areas where food is still available. For example, birds which breed in the forests of northern Europe and Asia move south to Africa and India in the autumn, returning in the following spring. These movements usually involve flights of considerable distances; for example, the eastern red-footed falcon flies from east Siberia to Southern Africa and back each year, a round trip of over 18,000 miles. Birds of prey often gather together to make these trips and will congregate at points where sea crossings are shortest. In Gibraltar, where the journey over the Mediterranean Sea to Africa is only fifteen miles, over 200,000 birds can be seen on their southerly autumn migration.

Bald eagles (below) stay in North America throughout the winter. Facing page: a common buzzard searches for rabbits in a Welsh valley.

6
Food

Above: a red-shouldered hawk struggles to swallow a snake. Golden eagles (below) will sometimes scavenge. The Everglades or snail kite (facing page top) feeds almost entirely on water snails. Facing page bottom: a Galápagos hawk devours a marine iguana.

Raptors are primarily *carnivorous*, and the group eats a wide range of foods including mammals, birds, amphibians, fish and *invertebrates*, while some even take vegetable matter and organic waste. Their food sources can vary in size from tiny termites to huge elephant carcasses, and many raptors are able to catch, kill and carry prey items much larger than themselves – pygmy falconets are champion weightlifters, being able to kill and carry birds over twice their size. Some species eat a wide variety of food, especially the scavengers, such as kites and vultures, which eat almost anything. Other birds of prey are specialized to catch and eat only a few, or even a single, species. Snail kites from the Americas eat only freshwater snails, which they winkle out of their shells with their extremely long upper beak, while African bat hawks hunt only at dusk, when they catch small bats which they swallow whole while still flying. Honey buzzards dig up the nests of wasps and bees to get the *grubs* and honeycombs they contain – for this purpose they have dense head feathers to protect them from the stings of irate bees and wasps which attack them as they dig.

7
Hunting Techniques

Most people are familiar with the sight of a kestrel hovering overhead, its wings beating rapidly as it searches for mice and voles, and then its swift plunge down into the grass onto the prey, but this is just one of a great many hunting techniques used by raptors.

Vultures search for dead animals. They soar on outstretched wings high up into the air, using warm *thermals* which rise from the African plains. As they slowly circle and spiral, they are able to scan large areas of land for carrion. Once a vulture spots a dead animal or notices other vultures on a kill, it drops down to the carcass in a steep glide at over a hundred miles per hour, and soon many vultures, often hundreds on a large carcass, gather to feed and fight over pieces of the body. Sometimes they eat so much that they cannot take off again and have to walk away until they have digested some of the food! New World vultures also "hunt" by sight in this way, but they can also smell rotting carcasses in the dense vegetation of the tropical forests where they live.

The lammergeier or "bone-breaker" is a type of vulture which feeds on the remains of dead animals after larger scavengers have had their fill. The large bones of these carcasses still contain food in the form of marrow, but they have to be broken up for this to become available. The lammergeier cannot break such bones in its beak, so instead it carries them high into the sky and then drops them onto rocks below, where they smash. It can then scrape out the marrow using its long, hard tongue. The Egyptian vulture has also developed a special way of getting more food. When it finds ostrich eggs, it picks up a stone in its beak and hurls it repeatedly at an egg until it shatters, enabling it to consume the contents. This is a rare example of a bird using a tool.

Many raptors hunt live prey from the air. Some use high, soaring flights to spot prey on

the ground. Then they dive down at great speed and snatch the prey before it sees them and can escape. This method is often used by raptors living in open country; for example, golden eagles use it when hunting rabbits, and African martial eagles adopt this method to catch small antelopes. Sometimes this rapid dive is directed at birds in flight. The peregrine falcon hunts pigeons and pheasants by rising above them and then folding its wings and dropping like a stone, hurtling towards the prey at great speeds. These dives are called stoops. A falcon hits the prey with its feet outstretched and with such force that the bird is usually killed outright and simply drops to the ground, where the falcon retrieves it. Other raptors hunt nearer the ground. The North American sharp-shinned hawk usually hunts small birds in woodland where visibility is low, so the prey is only sighted at close range. Once spotted, the hawk uses its quick acceleration and high maneuverability to chase the birds in a frantic, twisting rush in and out of trees and bushes.

Many species also hunt from perches, setting up ambushes in a concealed vantage point and waiting until prey stray within range. When the moment is right, the hawk dives onto the unsuspecting prey, usually pinning it to the ground. In the case of ospreys, the prey is not on

The crested baza (below) lives in Australia and feeds mainly on insects and frogs. Bottom left: white-backed and Ruppell's griffon vultures at a wildebeest carcass.

the ground but underwater. From its waterside perch, the osprey waits until a fish nears the surface, then it swoops off its perch toward the target, plunges feet first into the water and grapples the slippery fish with its long, sharp talons. The underside of an osprey's feet are covered in sharp spicules to increase its grip (like the treads on a car tire help to grip a slippery road). Once the fish is secure in these non-slip feet, the bird struggles away from the water to a perch, where it eats its hard-earned meal. Occasionally ospreys are drowned when they grab a fish too strong for them and are dragged underwater, being unable to release their grip to free themselves.

While many raptors eat their food on the ground, very few actually hunt on the ground. However, one which has specialized in this way of life is the secretary bird, which walks around the plains of Africa searching for snakes and small rodents. When it finds something to its liking, it kills it by stamping on it repeatedly with its long legs and strong feet. There are other species of raptor which also hunt on the ground some of the time. African harrier hawks from South Africa have long, slim legs which are double-jointed, so they can bend in all directions to probe deep into tree holes and rock crevices to search for prey, usually lizards.

The European sparrowhawk (facing page bottom left) feeds on a variety of songbirds, including great tits. Facing page bottom right: swooping low over a forest clearing, a red-tailed hawk hunts rodents and small birds.

8
Prey Handling

Many prey items, even quite large ones, are swallowed whole. Snake eagles, which have specially armored scales on their legs to protect them from poisonous snake bites, swallow snakes in one gulp, rather as we eat spaghetti. However, many raptors take considerable care preparing their food – usually the prey is taken to a safe place and all the indigestible materials, such as bones, fur, feathers or fish-scales are removed; debris which can be found in small piles under the perches where the hawk eats its meal. Then the prey is held in the feet and meat is pulled off the carcass with the beak. While eating, raptors hold their wings open over the prey like a cloak, shrouding the food from view – behavior known as mantling – which prevents the prey from being stolen by other birds.

Despite the care many birds take in preparing their meal, some indigestible material is usually eaten. This material collects in the *gizzard* where it forms into a pellet. This moist, slimy capsule of bones bound together with fur and feathers is then passed back up the throat and ejected or

Facing page: a tawny eagle perches near a dead European stork in Kenya. Ospreys (above) are specially adapted to catch fish, plunging into the water talons first to grab suitable prey. Below: a peregrine falcon plucks and eats a pigeon it has just killed. It hunts by diving at great speed onto unsuspecting prey.

cast through the mouth with a sharp cough, about twenty-four hours later.

9
Territories and Courtship

Most raptors are *monogamous*, and they mate for life, only seeking a new partner if their old one dies. If they are resident birds, the pair tend to stay together on a territory all year. But if they are migratory, they break up after breeding, migrate and live separately through the winter, only pairing up again when they return to the breeding territory in the spring.

A territory is an area of land which an animal will defend aggressively against other individuals, and within which it will breed and obtain food. Most raptors are territorial. Such territories can vary in size from a few square miles in the case of small accipiters, to over 150 square miles in the case of Verreaux's eagle.

It is during this establishment of breeding territories in the spring that most raptors perform their spectacular aerial displays for each other.

Courtship feeding on an Australian lake – a female white-breasted sea eagle arrives to retrieve a fish caught by her mate.

These show other raptors that the territory is occupied, and also help strengthen the bond between the pair. The main display is an undulating flight in which the male dives and swoops over the breeding territory, calling loudly. This usually deters an intruding bird. However, if the intruder continues into the territory, and especially if it approaches the nest site, the owner will give chase – and even fight viciously – to try to drive the intruder away.

Sometimes the female joins in the swooping display. The male often dive-bombs her with his talons lowered; the female then turns over in mid-air and raises her claws toward him, and occasionally the two interlock their talons and descend to the ground in a series of whirling somersaults and cartwheels. Such displays are not performed for fun, but demonstrate that the male has a territory and is ready to mate, and that the female is ready to accept him.

Food is involved in the courtship displays of certain raptors. Male ospreys carry fish in their talons and complete a series of steep dives and climbs to advertise themselves to potential mates. Male harriers carry food in the same manner, but instead they fly past their mates, dropping the food as they do so. The female has to fly upside-down in order to catch the food in mid-air. Such use of food in courtship displays allows the male to show the female how good he is at hunting.

Right: a pair of Madagascar kestrels struggle to maintain their balance while mating high in a tree, and (below) a pair of bald eagles lock talons and tumble through the air as part of their courtship and pair-bonding behavior.

10

From Nests to Nestlings

Most raptors build nests high in trees or on cliff ledges where they are safe from disturbance, but sometimes, where there are no high places, such as deserts, grassy plains and marshes, they nest on the ground. Only New World vultures and the falcons do not build nests. Instead, these birds use a hollow tree, or the nest of another bird, or else lay their eggs in a scrape of a cliff ledge or even directly on the ground.

Small raptors tend to build a new nest each year, while larger ones may return to the same nest year after year. In Scotland, the same cliff sites have been used for over a hundred years by numerous golden eagles and peregrines, while in South Africa a tree nest was used for over seventy years by various crowned eagles. These regularly-used nests, which are repaired and

Above: a lanner falcon chick struggling out of its egg, a process which takes many hours of effort. Below: high on an Alaskan cliff top, a bald eagle settles to incubate her eggs. These will hatch after about five weeks.

Ospreys (above left) return to nest at traditional sites year after year, adding material to the nest on each visit. This results in huge nests at some well used sites. Above: an osprey returns to its nest carrying lining material in its talons.

added to each year, can grow to enormous proportions. A golden eagle eyrie in Scotland was over fifteen feet in height and nearly six feet across. As they are added to each year, the weight of these nests becomes so great that eventually they snap the branches of the tree that supports them.

Many raptor species, especially the larger ones, only lay one or two eggs, and it is relatively rare to find any species laying more than five. The largest eggs are those of the Andean condor, which are six by three inches, the smallest are the pygmy falconet's, hardly bigger than a pea. Raptor eggs are usually light colored and spotted, having a reddish-brown pigment.

The eggs are laid at two to four day intervals. They must be kept warm if they are to hatch, so one of the parents (usually the female) sits on them and uses her body heat to maintain the temperature. *Incubation* starts as soon as the first egg is laid. In small falcons incubation lasts around fourteen days, while in eagles and condors it lasts up to fifty-two days. The eggs hatch in the order in which they were laid, and in most raptor species the young are raised together in a family group. However, in some eagle species, life for the eaglets is hard. These species usually lay two eggs, and by the time the second egg has hatched, the first hatched chick is several days old and quite large. In times of food shortage the larger chick may attack the smaller one, pecking it and chasing it around the nest. This harrassment usually results in the death of the younger chick, either from peck wounds or because it is so small that it is beaten to the food by its sibling and so starves. Usually the dead chick is then eaten by the older one.

11
Parental Care and the Chicks

The fledging period is the time spent by the young on the nest from hatching to first flight. For the small accipiters it lasts around twenty-four days, for large eagles 120 days, and for condors almost half a year!

When the chicks first hatch they are covered with a fine, silky down and their eyes are open. They are weak and helpless, and can only just lift their heads. Their lack of feathers means they have no protection from the weather and cannot keep themselves warm, so the female sits on them while their feathers grow, a process known as *brooding*. While the female spends all her day at the nest, the male is away hunting to provide food, not only for himself, but for his mate and young chicks as well. He has to hunt from dawn until dusk to catch enough food to keep his family alive, as the female only leaves the nest to collect food from the male. She brings this back to the nest, tears it up into bite-sized pieces and carefully feeds it to the young with her beak.

The chicks grow rapidly, and soon their downy coat is replaced by a thicker, woolly plumage which helps protect them from the weather. The chicks are now much stronger, more lively, and are able to shuffle unsteadily around the nest. At this stage they are still fed by

Above: a one-week-old bald eagle chick being delicately fed scraps of food by its mother. Facing page: half-grown red-tailed hawk chicks stand in the nest waiting for their parents to return with food. Their immature plumage is beginning to appear.

the female from food caught by the male, but as they grow larger and need more and more food the female starts to hunt as well, until soon she only broods them at night and during bad weather. By the end of this stage the chicks are strong enough and co-ordinated enough to stand, move around the nest quite actively, grab larger chunks of food from the female and try to feed themselves – although not always successfully at this stage.

As the chicks' wing and tail feathers begin to grow, their bodies become covered in immature, brown plumage. The chicks increase in strength and are very quick and active, running around the nest, fighting over any food the parents leave for them and starting to prepare for their first flight. Once their long wings and tail feathers finish growing, the young start to practice their flying movements by hopping up and down on the nest edge and frantically flapping their wings. Suddenly, and often by accident, as they stumble off the nest edge or are caught by a gust of wind, they launch into their first flight. This is usually awkward and ends in an unsteady landing just a little way from the nest.

Young, down-covered sparrowhawk chicks compete for food offered by their parent.

12
To Adulthood

Parental care for the young does not finish when the chicks leave the nest. Their flying ability and their hunting skills only improve with practice, and so, for a considerable period while the fledglings master these tasks, they depend on their parents for food. The parents take an active role in teaching these skills to the young birds. They play aerial games with the chicks that allow the youngsters to practice diving, twisting and chasing. They also force the young to chase them in order to obtain food, often dropping prey in mid-air for the young to catch. These games are a very important way of teaching the young how to survive. Eventually the fledglings start to catch some of their own food, but it may take a long time before they are completely able

An immature bald eagle has very different plumage from that of its parents.

to fend for themselves. In some birds this learning period may take only a few weeks, while in some eagles and condors it often takes over a year.

Once independent of the parents, the young birds are called immatures or juveniles. They live like adult birds except that they do not breed, and can be distinguished from the adults by their dull plumage. This period may be as short as nine months in small species like kestrels and sparrowhawks, or as long as four years in the larger eagles and seven years in condors. This is a very difficult time for the young birds, and many never reach their first birthday. Between fifty and seventy per cent die before they are able to breed, usually because of their inexperience. They may injure themselves when hunting, chase the wrong type of prey, try to live in the wrong places, or fall foul of other predators. If they make it through these difficult years, they then enter adulthood, pair up, occupy a territory and start to breed.

The large falconiformes are some of the longest-lived animals in the world. In captivity, many large raptors live to well over thirty years, and eagles and vultures for forty to fifty years. A bateleur which lived to a grand old age of fifty years is the oldest raptor on record.

Adult and immature bald eagles fight over a scrap of food. Many young raptors starve to death in their first winter because they have not yet perfected their hunting techniques.

13
Raptors and Man

As they are such efficient hunters, man has long made use of trained birds of prey to provide him with food or sport. The art of training hawks – falconry – commonly uses peregrines to hunt for pigeons and game birds, and goshawks to hunt for hares, rabbits and pheasants. Falconry originated in the Middle East and India around 4,000 years ago, and had spread to Europe by 500 AD. By the Middle Ages it had become a very important pastime, and many people had hawks, though only kings and knights could afford large birds. Today there are relatively few falconers in Europe, but it is still very popular in the Middle East, where huge prices are paid for the best birds.

Raptors are either taken from the nest as young birds or else trapped in nets as adults. To stop the bird from escaping, the falconer attaches leather thongs known as jesses to its legs, which are in turn tied to a leash, and a hood, or rufter, over its head to keep it calm. The bird is then trained to hunt for its keeper. Such training takes a very long time and requires much patience on the part of the falconer. First, the bird must get used to being handled and carried on the falconer's arm, which is protected from the bird's talons by a thick leather glove, and then it must also learn to take meat from the falconer's hand. Later it is taught to fly and retrieve meat while tied to a line to stop it flying away. Finally, it is tame enough to kill real prey and return to the falconer, who then collects his dinner.

In falconry, man and raptor work together, but in other instances man has caused serious harm to many raptor species. Although very strong and powerful, many raptors are easily hurt by humans. Even though raptors actually help man by killing pests, such as rats, or removing carrion from the land, they do occasionally kill animals which humans use –

A falconer with a golden eagle.

like sheep, poultry or game birds. As a result, raptors have been killed by man across the world.

In Britain, America and Australia many farmers used to believe that eagles killed large numbers of lambs, while in Canada bald eagles

The aerial spraying of crops with pesticides (top) has had very serious effects on the populations of many birds of prey. Above: a dead sparrowhawk hung up on a gamekeeper's gibbet.

were blamed for eating too many salmon and affecting the fishermen's catches. Farmers and fishermen shot eagles as pests, and they even paid *bounties* for dead eagles. In this century alone, nearly 130,000 bald eagles were shot in Alaska, and 150,000 wedge-tailed eagles were killed in Australia. At one time the killing of all raptors was accepted practice, and many populations were almost totally destroyed. It has been estimated that several million raptors of all kinds were killed in Europe between 1950 and 1970.

Research eventually showed that, in most cases, raptors had little effect on the populations they were accused of destroying. For instance, eagles were not killing lambs, but acting as scavengers and feeding on lambs which had already died. As a result of these findings, many raptor species are now protected by laws, and in some places their populations are returning to their old levels. In recent years man has even helped to re-establish raptor populations in areas where they had disappeared, for example sea eagles from Scandinavia have been released in Scotland, while bald eagles have been reintroduced into the eastern United States.

A more indirect effect man has had on raptors comes from the use of poisonous chemicals called pesticides, which are used by farmers to kill insect pests on their crops. As small animals eat the crops, and the chemical run-off from the fields enters rivers, these poisons are taken in by mammals and fish, which are in turn eaten by raptors. The more contaminated prey raptors eat, the more poisons they accumulate, until they themselves are poisoned. These chemicals also have other effects. Female raptors poisoned by pesticides lay eggs with such thin shells that they simply smash when the female tries to sit on them. In addition, chemical contamination can also cause chicks to die before they hatch.

When raptors suffer such chemical poisoning, no new birds are produced to replace those which die, and so their numbers start to fall. During the 1960s such effects were responsible for the near extinction of sparrowhawks and peregrine falcons in many areas of Britain and Europe, and peregrines and bald eagles in many areas of America. The use of these chemicals has now been banned by law in many areas, and species have begun to recover and recolonize areas where they were previously extinct.

Perhaps the most serious threat to worldwide raptor populations is that of habitat destruction. The continued growth and development of human populations and man's need for natural resources means that there is an ever-increasing loss of unspoiled habitats. Many raptors are very large birds and need big areas in which to hunt, so when people destroy forests or take land to build on, these birds are the first to suffer. Thus, to protect a species we cannot simply save the animals, we must preserve their habitat as well.

We should strive to protect these birds, not only because they are exciting, powerful and beautiful, but, because they are extremely sensitive to any deterioration in their environment, they can show us when our own environment is threatened.

Below: the rare black and white hawk eagle of South America, threatened by the loss of forests in its range. Nearly wiped out by the effects of poisonous chemicals, the peregrine falcon (bottom) was re-introduced after captive breeding.

Glossary

ACCIPITER – hawk with short, rounded wings and a long tail.

BOUNTY – sum paid for killing an animal that is considered dangerous or a pest.

BROODING – (of birds) parent protecting and keeping chicks warm by covering them with its body.

CARNIVOROUS – meat eating.

DORMANT – inactive, like being asleep.

ENTRAILS – intestines and other internal body organs.

GIZZARD – (of bird) the second stomach used to grind up food.

GRUBS – (of insects) the larval stage of development (maggots).

HIBERNATE – to spend a cold period in a dormant state.

INCUBATION – (of birds) the warming of eggs by an adult sitting on them.

INVERTEBRATES – animals without backbones, such as worms and insects.

MONOGAMOUS – having one mate at a time.

PREDATOR – an animal that hunts other animals for food.

PREENING – action of birds as they clean and arrange feathers with their beaks.

ROOST – (of birds) a perching or resting place.

TEMPERATE – (of weather) neither very hot nor very cold.

THERMALS – rising currents of heated air.

Picture Credits

Tony Allen 24 *bottom*; Mike Birkhead 19 *bottom*, 30 *bottom*; Patricia Caulfield/ANIMALS ANIMALS 15 top; David Cayless 7 *bottom*, 17 *bottom*; Judd Cooney 23 *left*; Michael Fogden 5 *top*; D.G. Fox 22 *top*; Jim Frazier 17 *right*; Frank Huber 10; Lon Lauber 1, 2, 5 *bottom*, 9, 11, 22 *bottom*, 24 *top*, 27; Michael Leach, 13, 16 *left*; Aldo Brando Leon 31 top; Ted Levin/ANIMALS ANIMALS 23 *left*; Tony Martin 7 *top*; Godfrey Merlen 15 *bottom*; Stan Osolinski 4, 8 *top*, 14 *top*, 19 *top*; Charles Palek/ANIMALS ANIMALS 25; Mark Pidgeon 21 top; Edwin Sadd 8 *right*, 18; C.W. Schwartz/ANIMALS ANIMALS 16 *right*; Wendy Shattil and Bob Rozinski 12, 21 *bottom*, 26, 31 *bottom*; Alastair Shay 6, 28, 29; Tim Shepherd 30 *top*; Tom Ulrich 14 *bottom*; Belinda Wright 20.